CHURCHES

IONA

DURHAM

FOUNTAINS ABBEY

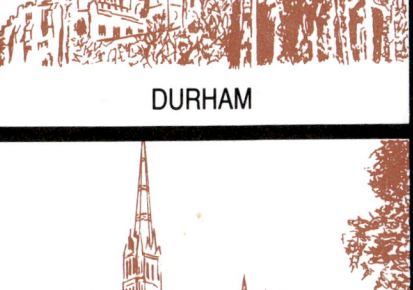
CANTERBURY

SALISBURY

YORK

ST DAVID'S

WESTMINSTER ABBEY

ST GEORGE'S CHAPEL

KING'S COLLEGE CHAPEL

ST PAUL'S

WESLEY'S CHAPEL

WESTMINSTER CATHEDRAL

COVENTRY

LIVERPOOL RC CATHEDRAL

Stonehenge from a drawing by J. M. W. Turner

GREAT BRITISH MONUMENTS

The Diagram Group

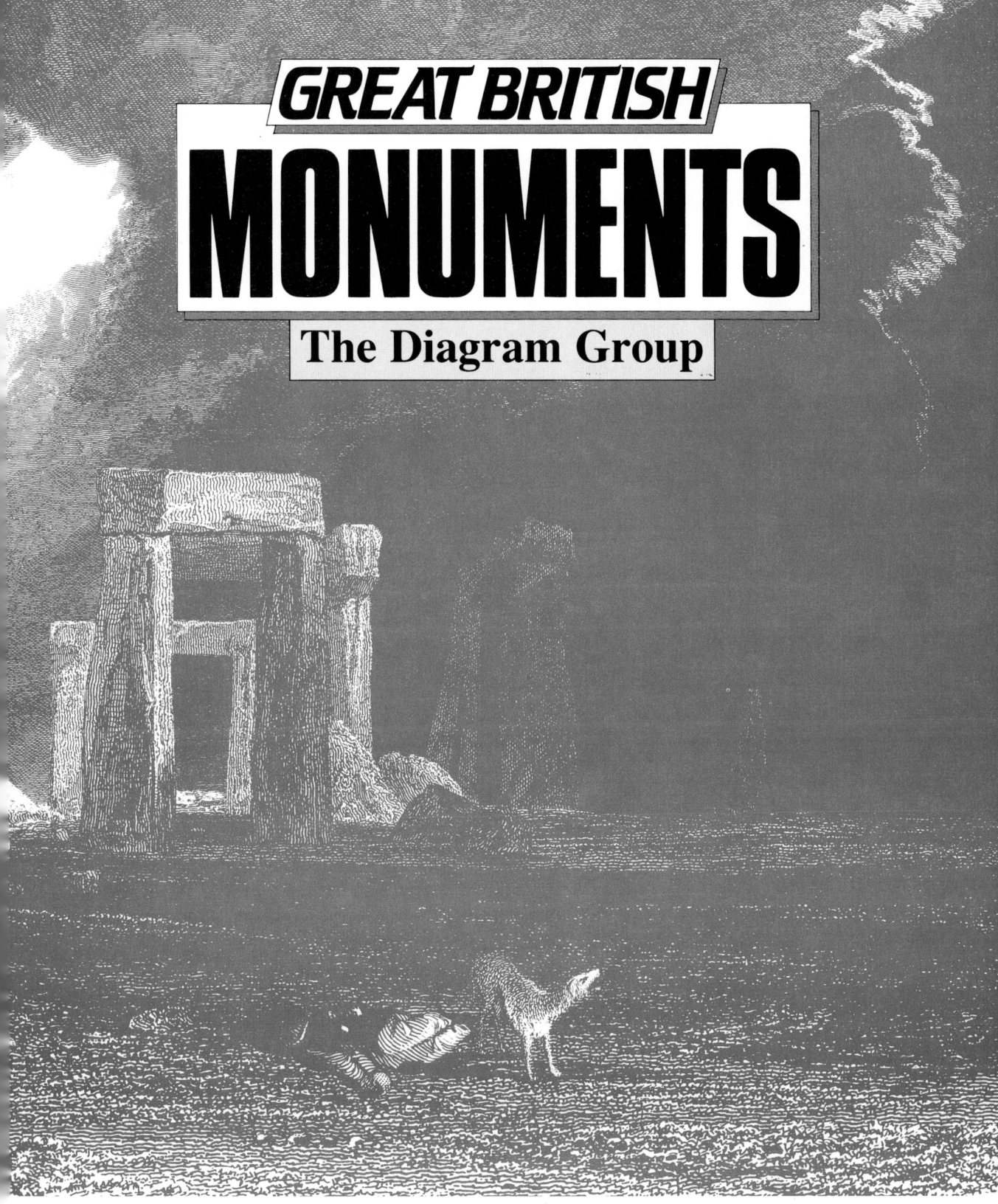

Franklin Watts
London New York Sydney Toronto

Acknowledgements
Picture Research: Patricia Robertson
Cover: ZEFA
Title page: Mansell Collection
Aerofilms 9
BBC Hulton Picture Library 19, 35
Bedford County Press 23
British Tourist Authority 7, 31
Mansell Collection 12, 13, 18, 20, 24, 25, 26-27, 28-29, 33
National Trust for Scotland 14-15
Royal British Legion 32
Royal Commission for the Ancient and Historical Monuments of Scotland 17

Contents

Monuments through the ages	4
Stonehenge	6
White Horse of Uffington	8
Eleanor of Castile Crosses	10
The Monument	12
Glenfinnan Monument	14
The Scott Monument	16
Nelson's Column	18
Marble Arch	20
Ickwell Green Maypole	22
The Albert Memorial	24
Cleopatra's Needle	26
Drake's Statue	28
Eros	30
The Cenotaph	32
Churchill's Statue	34
Monuments of interest	36
Types of monuments	38
Useful addresses	40
Index	41

© Diagram Visual Information Ltd 1987

First published in Great Britain 1987 by
Franklin Watts Ltd
12a Golden Square
London W1R 4BA

Printed in France

ISBN 0 86313 457 2

Monuments through the ages

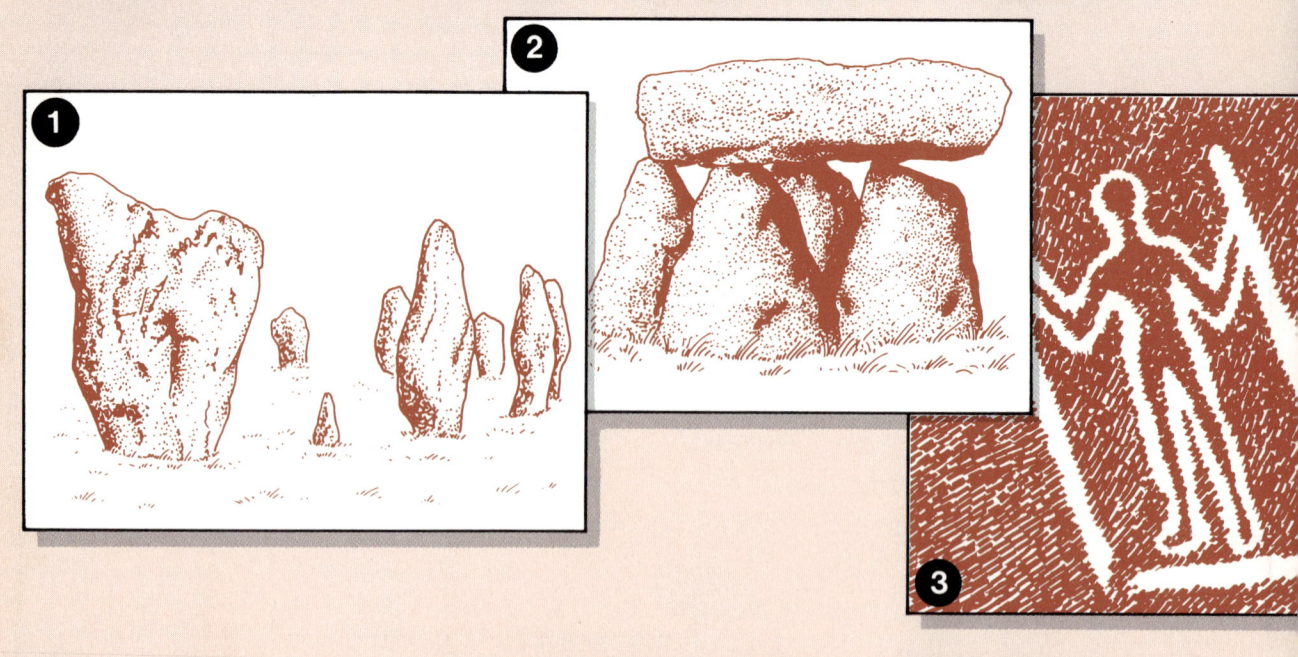

Some examples of monuments from prehistoric to modern times:
1 A stone circle.
2 A dolmen or burial chamber.
3 A chalk-cut figure.
4 A Celtic cross.
5 Hadrian's Wall.
6 An obelisk commemorating an event.
7 Statue of King Alfred.
8 Cross at Flodden Field.
9 Mausoleum, a burial place.

10 A market cross.
11 A brass in a church.
12 A victory column.
13 A triumphal arch.
14 A public drinking fountain.
15 A blue plaque on a building.
16 A commemorative sculpture.

Stonehenge

A reconstruction of how Stonehenge would have looked with the circle of 30 standing stones capped with lintels and the horseshoe of five trilithons.

Almost everything about Stonehenge is shrouded in mystery. For more than 4,500 years, huge stones have been standing in the middle of Salisbury Plain in Wiltshire. Nobody knows who put them there, or how about 100 stones were carried to the site before the wheel was invented.

It is believed to be the greatest Bronze Age temple in Europe, but we have little idea of the cultures that erected this over a period of 1,000 years, or the religion of the people who worshipped there. It was already in ruins when the Druid priests arrived in Britain, so they did not worship there.

Archaeologists have discovered that Stonehenge was started in the Stone Age and built in four

Stonehenge as it is today. The size of the stones is still very impressive.

stages. In its earliest form, it was a large, circular earthwork (a henge), 116m (380ft) in diameter. A huge stone called the Heel Stone was set outside the circle. It lined up with the opening to the bank where people assembled.

Stonehenge reached its final stage in about 1500 BC, and we can see the ruins of this today. The most remarkable feature was the outer circle of 30 standing stones with lintels. The circle enclosed a horseshoe of five trilithons (two upright stones with a lintel on top). Each stone was about 2m (7ft) wide and 4m (14ft) high. Some weighed over 20 tons and were brought from Marlborough Downs, twenty miles away, probably on rollers.

Enough of these stones remain in place to give modern visitors some sense of the awe and magic that Stonehenge held. At dawn on the longest day of the year, anyone standing at the centre of the monument will see the sun rise over the Heel Stone beyond the encircling bank.

c 2500 BC
Stone Age people raised circular earth bank
c 2100 BC
Bronze Age people put ring of Welsh bluestones inside circular bank
c 2000 BC
Bluestones replaced by larger sarsen stones. Standing stones placed inside ring. Axe heads carved on stone
c 1550 BC
Bluestone circle added to centre. Altar stone set up
c 300 BC
Iron Age Celts and their Druid priests arrived in Britain. Stonehenge already in ruins

White Horse of Uffington

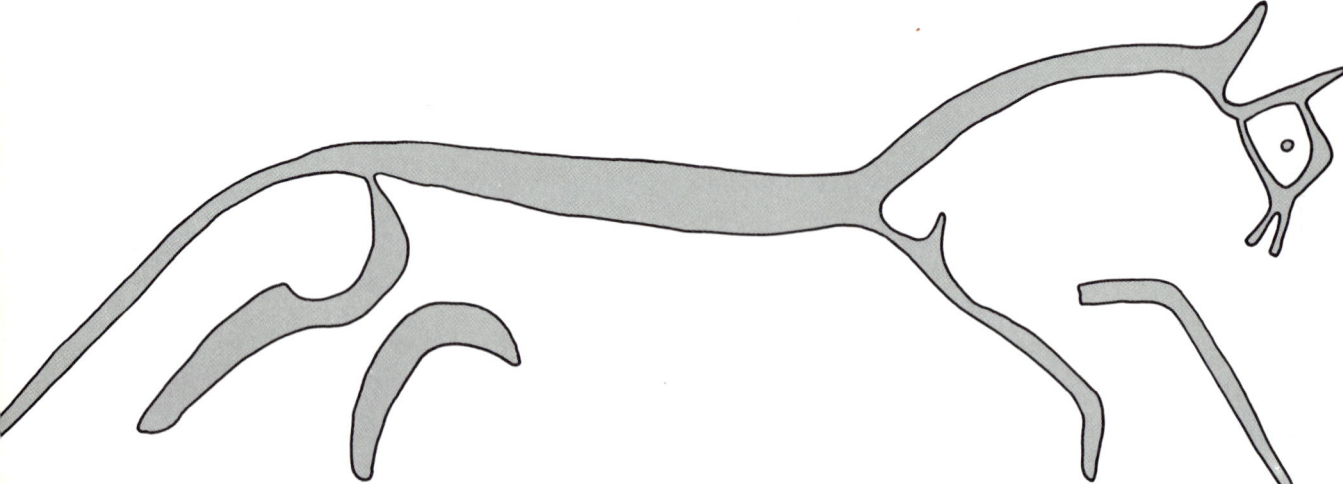

The White Horse at Uffington has been known as a horse for 900 years. Some have suggested that the disjointed body, long tail and beaked jaw could be that of a dragon.

c 100 BC
White Horse carved into hillside
AD 303
St George died in Palestine
c 1084
White Horse Hill mentioned in writings
1190
Site described as the hill where one climbs the White Horse
1857
Last scouring ceremony
1892
White Horse listed as ancient monument
1940
White Horse covered over during the war to stop enemy aircraft using it as a landmark

The White Horse of Uffington is the oldest and the largest of Britain's hill figures. Its disjointed figure was formed by cutting off the top layer of turf and showing the white chalk below of the Berkshire Downs. From nose to tail it measures about 114m (374ft) and stands 39m (130ft) tall.

Nobody knows when or why it was cut into the hillside. One theory is that it was carved by Iron Age Celtic tribesmen in the 1st or 2nd century BC. They were great horsemen and were known to worship a horse goddess called Epona. As the horse can be seen from 20 miles away, it showed that they occupied this area. They lived in an Iron Age hill fort called Uffington Castle, just above the horse.

Another theory is that it was carved to commemorate the victory over the Danes in 871 by Alfred the Great, king of England from 871-899. He was known to have a white horse on his banner, but this faced to the left and not the right. The Celtic horse faced right.

Near the White Horse are terraces on the hills called Giant's Stairs and Dragon's Hill. This is where, according to local legend, St George killed the dragon. There are bare patches where no grass will grow because the dragon's blood fell there.

There used to be a celebration every seven years called 'The Scouring of the Horse'. It lasted for two days and the horse was cleaned and weeded. There was music, dancing, games, sideshows and feasting. It was stopped in 1857 because churchmen complained that it was a pagan custom. The horse was last traditionally scoured in 1884. Since then local people have always kept the figure clean. It takes four men three weeks to complete the job.

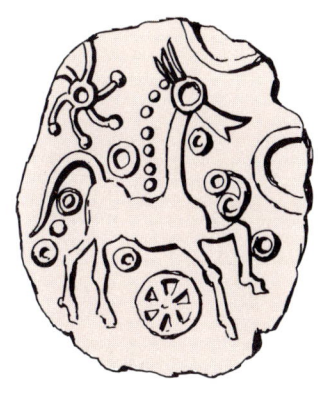

An Iron Age coin showing a horse facing to the right. Some coins were very similar to the Uffington horse.

An aerial view of the hillside. Dragon's Hill is at the bottom front of the picture. The Giant's Stairs are below the horse and its nose points to the hill fort.

Eleanor of Castile Crosses

The Eleanor Crosses were set up by King Edward I as a memorial to his wife, Queen Eleanor of Castile. Eleanor always accompanied her husband on his travels. They were returning to Scotland in 1290 when Eleanor became ill. She died at Harby in Nottinghamshire. The king ordered the body to be brought back to Westminster Abbey for burial. The funeral procession took 12 days to reach London. The following year, the king decided that 12 crosses should be put up to mark each of the places where the coffin rested overnight.

The three crosses that survive at Geddington, Hardingstone and Waltham Cross.

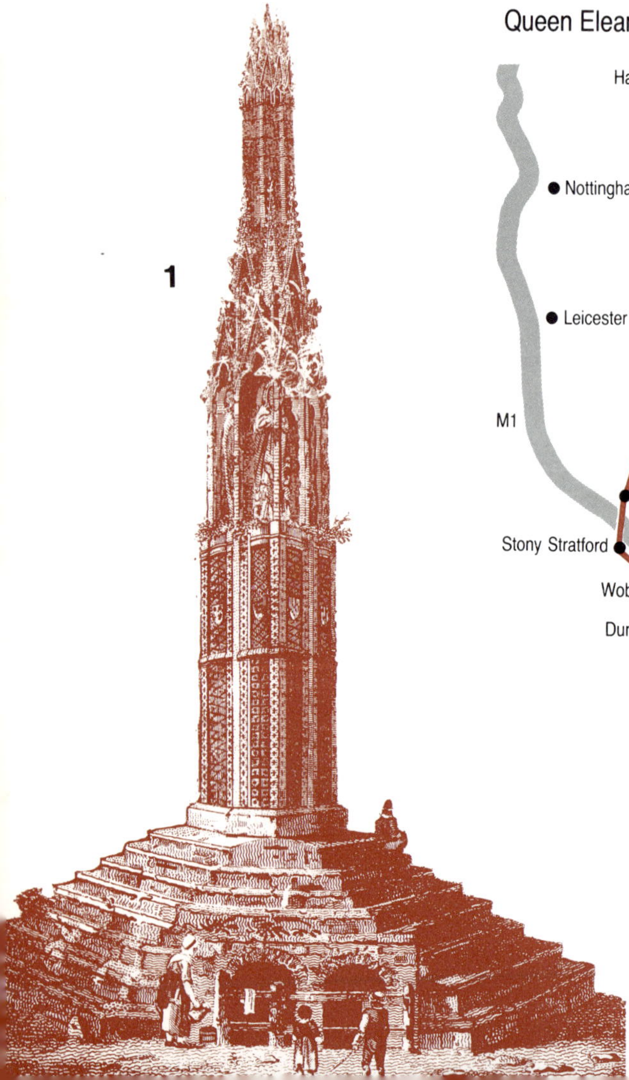

Queen Eleanor's last journey

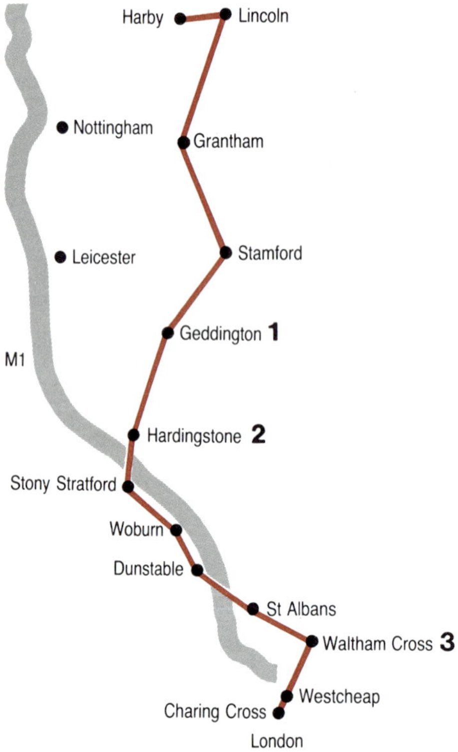

The gilded bronze effigy of Queen Eleanor which lies on her tomb in Westminster Abbey. It was cast by William Torel, a goldsmith. The tomb is made of Purbeck marble.

3

The crosses were designed and sculpted by different artists. Each monument had steps round the base and niches where statues of the queen were placed. A cross was put on the top. They were all completed by 1295 but only three have survived. The best preserved is the cross at Geddington in Northamptonshire, but nobody knows who created the monument with its delicate stonework. The court sculptors could not produce as many as 12 quickly, so it was probably made by sculptors in the area. The cross at Hardingstone has eight sides. It is the work of John of Battle and the statues are by William of Ireland. The Waltham Cross has six sides and was made by court artists.

The most famous cross no longer exists. It was set up in the village of Ceirring, next to Westminster where the queen was to be buried. It was removed by an act of parliament in 1647. However in 1863, when the site of the village had become the railway terminus for the London, Chatham and Dover Railway Company, they ordered a new cross to be put on the site. It stands in the forecourt of what is now Charing Cross station in London.

1290
Queen Eleanor died
1291
King Edward commissioned 12 crosses
1292
Hardingstone cross brought from London
1293
Life-size statue of Queen Eleanor placed at grave in Westminster Abbey
1647
Charing Cross destroyed by order of parliament
1863
New cross erected by railway company
1890
Repairs made to Waltham Cross

Monument

An engraving of the Great Fire of London, from a painting done at the time of the fire.

1666
Great Fire of London
1671-77
Monument erected
1788
First suicide from balcony
1825
Monument illuminated with portable gas to mark start of work on London Bridge
1842
Balcony enclosed after sixth suicide
1954
Stone cleaned, urn re-gilded

The Monument is the tallest isolated single column in the world. It was built as a reminder of the Great Fire of London which broke out on 2nd September, 1666, in a baker's shop at the corner of Pudding Lane. It stands over 61m (202ft) high and the height of the Monument is the exact distance from the shop where the fire first started. The fire raged for five days and destroyed 89 churches, 400 streets and 13,200 houses, as well as all the other public buildings. An act of parliament was passed to provide for the city to be rebuilt and for a memorial to the Great Fire to be erected in Fish Street.

The Monument was designed by the architect, Sir Christopher Wren, working with the inventor, Robert Hooke. It is built of Portland stone. Some of the original inscriptions on the base have been removed. There are raised carvings round the base

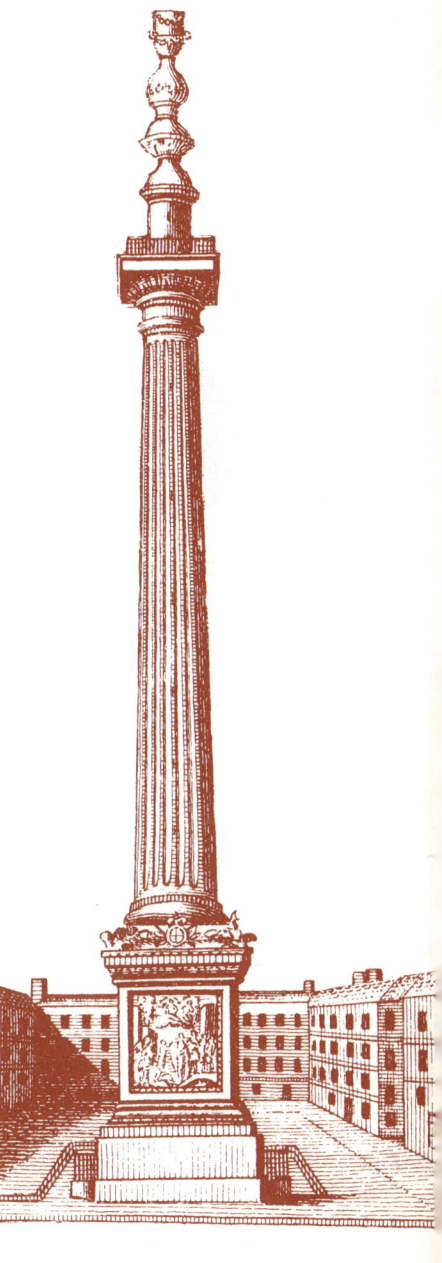

After the sixth person committed suicide by jumping from the gallery, it was closed and a cage put round it.

The Monument in Fish Street.

showing London destroyed and restored, and Charles II urging people on with the rebuilding. Wren had wanted a statue of Charles II at the top with brass flames climbing up the tower, but this was not approved. At the top is a flaming urn of gilt bronze to symbolise the fire.

Below the urn is a balcony. To reach this there is a spiral staircase with 311 steps. When the Monument was completed, it was used by members of the Royal Society for astronomical purposes. They found that when wagons rolled past it vibrated too much so their observations could not be accurate. The balcony gives a splendid view over the city of London but after six people had committed suicide by jumping from this, the staircase was closed while a metal cage was built round the balcony to stop people jumping off.

Glenfinnan Monument

1745
Bonnie Prince Charlie returned from France and landed in Scotland. Standard raised at Glenfinnan on 19th August
1746
Scots defeated at Culloden Moor; Bonnie Prince Charlie left Scotland
1815
Monument raised
1834
Statue by John Greenshield placed on top
1938
Presented to National Trust for Scotland

At Glenfinnan in the Western Highlands, at the head of Loch Shiel, stands a tall stone column with a kilted Highlander on top. It marks the spot where the Scottish clans gathered on 19th August 1745 to support Prince Charles Edward Stuart, known as Bonnie Prince Charlie. He had come back from France, where he had been living in exile, to plan a campaign to regain the throne of Great Britain and Ireland for the Royal House of Stuart.

For two days councils of war were held and provisions organised and arms and ammunition distributed. Then the Highland army set off from Glenfinnan to march eastwards. They had hoped to get support from France but this did not arrive. They gathered recruits on the way. After the victory in September at Prestonpans they were 5,000 in number. In October Bonnie Prince Charlie stayed at Holyroodhouse and from there

The superb setting at Glenfinnan at the head of Loch Shiel. The island on the loch is St Finnan's Isle, the burial place of the Macdonalds.

set out for London. When he was within 100 miles of London he was persuaded to retreat. At a battle at Culloden Moor in the following April, the army was finally defeated. Bonnie Prince Charlie fled and returned to France.

In 1815, Alexander Macdonald ordered the stone tower to be built. His grandfather had been one of the clansmen to join the rising of 1745. An inscription in Gaelic, Latin and English commemorates the zeal, bravery and fidelity of the men who fought and died in the rising. In 1845, and again in 1945, thousands of people gathered at the Glenfinnan Monument to remember the loyal clansmen. Nowadays, on the Saturday nearest 19th August each year, the Glenfinnan Gathering and Highland Games are held. The full story of the campaign from Glenfinnan to Culloden is on view at the visitor centre at Glenfinnan.

A coin commemorating the Rising of 'Forty-Five when Prince Charles Edward Stuart was proclaimed Prince of Wales.

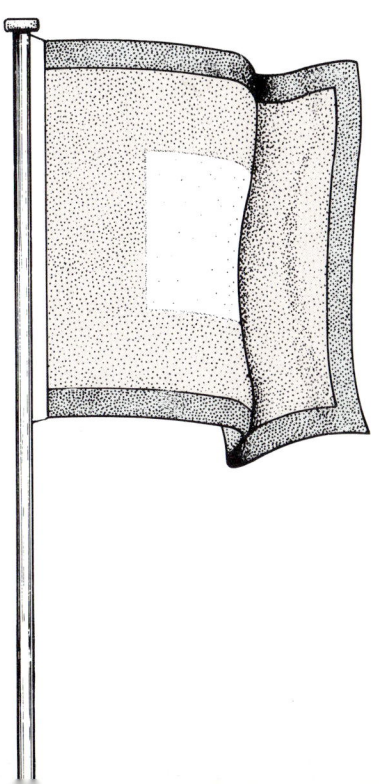

The Raising of the Standard at Glenfinnan. It was made of red silk, with a blue border and white centre.

Scott Monument

Sir Walter Scott

15 August 1771
Walter Scott born in Edinburgh
1786
Began legal training
1792
Called to Scottish bar
1797
Married Charlotte Carpenter
1802
First novel published
1820
Received knighthood
1826
Involved in bankruptcy cases
21 September 1832
Died at Abbotsford
1840-44
Memorial spire erected
1846
Scott Monument unveiled

The Scott Monument, a Gothic fantasy, is the only significant work known to be by Kemp.

The Scott Monument in Princes Street, Edinburgh, is a Gothic fantasy in memory of one of Scotland's best-known writers, Sir Walter Scott. A competition was held for the design of a monument. It was won by George Meikle Kemp, a self-taught architect and stonemason, who submitted his entry under another name. It is probably the largest monument to a writer anywhere in the world. The spire above the elaborate canopy rises to a height of about 60m (200ft). There are 64 statuettes of characters from Scott's novels. About eight months before the monument was finished, the designer fell into a canal and drowned, so never saw it unveiled.

The statue of Sir Walter Scott with his dog, Maida, was sculpted by Sir John Steell. It was installed in 1846, two years after the monument was built. The unveiling took place on August 15th, Scott's birthday.

Sir Walter Scott was born in Edinburgh in 1771. As a young man, he began writing even though he had qualified as a lawyer. His first novel, *Border Minstrelsy,* was an instant success, but he is best known for his Waverley novels. He became a partner in the printing and publishing companies which handled his books. In 1826, however, the firms became bankrupt and Scott found that he was responsible for their large debts. He started writing to try and earn enough money to pay off these debts. In six years he had paid back a considerable sum but his health was failing. He went abroad to try to restore his health. When he reached Rome, he realised he was not going to get better, so he returned to Scotland, where he died in 1832.

Nelson's Column

Sir Edwin Landseer modelling the lions which stand on the four corners of Nelson's Column.

The column was finished a year before the statue and scaffolding was put round the column so that the statue of Nelson could be placed on top.

29 September 1758
Horatio Nelson born in Norfolk
1771
Joined first ship
1779
Given first command
1787
Married Frances Nisbet
1798
Battle of the Nile
1805
Battle of Trafalgar; Nelson died
1830
Trafalgar Square named
1839-42
Granite column built
1843
Nelson statue put on column
1867
Bronze lions placed in position
1939
Fountains in square redesigned by Sir Edwin Lutyens

Nelson's Column is a tribute to Horatio Nelson. He joined the navy as a young boy and was given his first command of a frigate when he was only 20. He became one of Britain's most popular and successful naval commanders. The monument to him towers above any other statue in one of London's most famous squares, Trafalgar Square. It was named after the Battle of Trafalgar which took place off the southern tip of Spain. It was a great victory for Nelson against the French and Spanish fleets. Lord Nelson died of his wounds there but his body was brought back and he is buried in St Paul's Cathedral.

A committee was set up to raise funds for the monument and a competition was held for the design. It was won by the architect William Railton. The column is made of Devon granite and is about 52m (107ft) high. The statue of Nelson on top is over 5m (17ft) high. The plinth,

Trafalgar Square has become a well-known rallying place for public meetings and demonstrations.

Trafalgar Square decked with garlands for Trafalgar Day on 21st October, the anniversary of the Battle of Trafalgar.

the pedestal on which the column stands, is decorated with carvings cast from bronze which was melted down from captured French cannons. They show Nelson's major victories at the Battle of St Vincent, the Battle of the Nile, the Battle of Copenhagen and the Battle of Trafalgar. The four lions were added later. They were the work of Queen Victoria's favourite animal artist, Sir Edwin Landseer.

The platform between the lions is now used by speakers at public rallies and the square is famous for political demonstrations. The pigeons which are a familiar sight in the square rest on Nelson's statue. For Christmas, a huge tree is sent by the people of Norway. It is lit up and carols are sung. On New Year's Eve thousands of people gather in the square, and many end up in the fountains.

Marble Arch

Tyburn, the public execution place. Thousands flocked to see the condemned hanged, drawn and quartered before they were beheaded.

1196
First known execution at Tyburn
1571-1759
Permanent gallows, the Tyburn Tree, stood on site
1783
Last execution at Tyburn
1818
Marble Arch installed at Buckingham Palace
1851
Arch moved to present site
1908
Park railings moved to allow traffic past
1960
More roadworks making traffic island

Marble Arch was designed by John Nash for George IV. It stood in the forecourt of Buckingham Palace and was the special entrance for the sovereign and royal family. It was modelled on the triumphal Arch of Constantine in Rome. It is made of marble and has many sculptures. The top was supposed to be decorated with a band of sculptures but these were used on Buckingham Palace instead. A statue of George IV on horseback was intended to be placed on top, but this stands in Trafalgar Square.

When the East Front of Buckingham Palace, with the famous balcony, was built, the arch was no longer needed. It is said that it was too narrow for the state coach to pass through it. The arch was moved to its present position in the north-east corner of Hyde Park. The wrought iron gates are still kept closed and only the royal family and members of the King's Troop Royal Horse

Marble Arch, which stands in solitary splendour, on a traffic island at the top of London's busy Park Lane.

Artillery are allowed to pass through the gates.

In 1908, the park railings were moved back to allow traffic to move on the park side of Marble Arch. In 1960 another road was built and Marble Arch now stands on an island. This was the site of Tyburn where for 600 years prisoners were publicly executed. Many people gathered to see the condemned hanged, drawn and quartered. The Tyburn Tree, a permanent gallows, stood there for many years. The spot is marked in the roadway.

Just inside the park railings is Speakers' Corner. Since 1872 any member of the public has been allowed to stand on a soapbox and make a speech for anyone to hear. It is also the starting point for many protest marches. People rally in Hyde Park and march round Marble Arch either to Downing Street or Trafalgar Square.

Speaker's Corner, just inside Hyde Park, is a popular place for free speech on Sundays.

Ickwell Green Maypole

The maypole at Ickwell Green in Bedfordshire is one of the most famous in the country. May Day celebrations have been in existence for over four centuries. There are no records of when they started but the churchwarden's accounts in 1563 included money given towards the cost of Morris dancers' shoes. In 1565 they were stopped by puritans who thought it a pagan ritual.

The custom at Ickwell Green was revived in 1660. In 1850, villagers used to grease the pole and hang prizes from it about half way up. This was stopped as the pole became unsafe. Since 1872, a permanent red and white pole has been erected on one side of the huge village green. Before that, it was the custom to put up a pole on the first day of May each year.

May Day celebrations originally took the form of tree worship round a white hawthorn or may tree. Later, leafy branches were pinned at the top of the maypole. Now it is decorated with red and white ribbons. The primitive belief was that a kindly tree spirit lived in the tree and had the power to grant blessings and make the crops grow. Planting a may tree on the village green was thought to benefit all the inhabitants of the village.

Three neighbouring villages of Upper Caldecote, Old Warden and Northill join with Ickwell Green for the celebrations. Adults and children dress up in traditional costumes and sing and dance around the maypole. There are side shows and tea tents and the highlight is the crowning of the May Queen, chosen from the village girls. The whole village is on holiday for the day.

15th century
Villagers from Northill flee to Ickwell Green to avoid the Black Death
1565
May Day celebrations stopped by puritans
1660
Celebrations revived
1872
First permanent maypole set up on green

Kate Greenaway's illustration of children dancing round a may tree.

Dancing round the maypole used to be done by children only. Now customs have changed and adults take part. Morris dancers also form part of the festivities on May Day.

Albert Memorial

Queen Victoria ordered many memorials to Prince Albert but the best known is the national one in Kensington Gardens, opposite the Albert Hall in London. The Albert Memorial was designed by George Gilbert Scott. It took over ten years to build, but he received a knighthood for his work.

It is a splendid example of Victorian Gothic work. It reaches a height of 53m (175ft). On the corners are groups of statues representing the continents of Europe, America, Africa and Asia. The plinth, on which the memorial stands, has 24 steps which lead to the gun-metal statue of Prince Albert. It is 4.2m (14ft) high and shows him reading a copy of the Great Exhibition catalogue. Prince Albert had been closely involved with the Great Exhibition of 1851. The memorial stands on a site just west of where it was held.

Around the base of the memorial are 169 life-

To appreciate the work of the artists and craftsmen involved, you have to go up close to the memorial.

Prince Albert, named Prince Consort in 1857, had been of great help to Queen Victoria as an adviser and was sadly missed.

size figures of painters, architects, musicians, poets and sculptors and they are all named. Above them, on the corners, are statues representing agriculture, manufacture, commerce and engineering. There are more statues on the pillars and, under the cross, statues for Faith, Hope, Charity and Humility. The materials used on the memorial included granite, sandstone, limestone, slate, marble and mosaics. The spire is lead, inlaid with semi-precious stones. It cost £120,000 to build.

Prince Albert was a man of wide interests and the memorial echoes many of these. He was more popular than people realised and, when he died at the early age of 42, he was sadly missed. He influenced Queen Victoria a great deal and, throughout her long widowhood, she always acted as Prince Albert would have wished.

1819
Prince Albert of Saxe-Coburg-Gotha born
1840
Queen Victoria and Prince Albert married
1861
Prince Albert died at Windsor
1864
Foundations of national memorial laid
1872
Memorial opened to view; George Gilbert Scott knighted
1875
Statue of Prince Albert put in place
1876
The Albert Memorial unveiled

Two of the corner groups of marble statues representing Asia, with the elephant, and Africa, with the camel.

Cleopatra's Needle

The cylindrical pontoon being built round the obelisk.

Engineers shifting Cleopatra's Needle on the beach at Alexandria.

c 1450 BC
Obelisks brought to Heliopolis
c 44 BC
Moved to Alexandria
1819
Presented to George IV by Egyptian viceroy; offered again to William IV
1877
Towed out to sea
1878
Placed on embankment
1881
Bronze sphinxes by George Vulliamy set in place
1917
Sphinxes damaged by bombs during war

Cleopatra's Needle stands on the Thames Embankment in London. It is a granite obelisk about 18m (60ft) high and weighs 186 tons. It was cut in about 1475 BC from quarries in Egypt and moved from Aswan along the River Nile to Heliopolis. At this time there were two obelisks. The second one stands in Central Park in New York.

The Roman Emperor, Augustus Caesar, moved the obelisk to the city of Alexandria on the coast. Until then it had not been associated with Cleopatra. Her name was added about this time. It stood there for centuries until it fell over in the sand. It was still lying there when it was first offered to Britain in 1819. It was thought to be too difficult to move. In the 1870s General Sir James Alexander asked the engineer John Dixon, who was in Alexandria, to try and solve the problem.

Dixon built an iron cylindrical pontoon round

The obelisk being towed in stormy seas on its way from Egypt to England.

Cleopatra's Needle as it stands on the embankment in London. Originally it had no connection at all with Cleopatra.

the obelisk and it was towed out to sea. It was an eventful journey. Off the coast of Spain, there was a violent storm. Six seamen were killed and the obelisk was almost abandoned. It was recovered and towed to a Spanish port. It finally reached London in 1878. An inscription acknowledges the generosity of a famous Victorian surgeon, Erasmus Wilson, who paid for the obelisk to be brought to England.

Cleopatra's Needle was intended to stand in front of the Houses of Parliament. The land, however, was not solid enough to take the weight. The obelisk was moved to the embankment. It is guarded by two bronze sphinxes. Underneath Cleopatra's Needle is a time capsule containing objects of the day including a newspaper, a set of coins, a railway guide, bibles in different languages, photographs and children's toys.

Drake's Statue

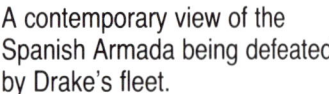

A contemporary view of the Spanish Armada being defeated by Drake's fleet.

The statue of Sir Francis Drake was erected at Plymouth Hoe 300 years after he returned from his round the world voyage.

In 1577 Francis Drake set sail from Plymouth in the *Pelican* and four other ships for an expedition to the Pacific to plunder Spanish ships. The winds separated the fleet. Drake's ship, renamed the *Golden Hind*, sailed south west across the Pacific while the rest of the fleet returned to England. Drake ended up being the first Englishman to sail round the world. The voyage took three years and he returned to Plymouth with a ship full of booty. He was knighted by Queen Elizabeth I for his achievements.

Drake was also famous for leading the defeat of the Spanish Armada in 1588. The story goes that he was playing bowls on Plymouth Hoe when the enemy fleet was sighted. He finished his game saying he had time to play and defeat the Spanish. In 1582 Drake was voted mayor of Plymouth. He became an admiral and continued fighting the Spanish for possessions in the West Indies. He died of a fever in Panama when he was leading his second campaign there.

The people of Plymouth decided to erect a statue to commemorate the third centenary of Drake's safe return from his round the world voyage. Meanwhile, the people of Tavistock, where Drake was born, were also planning a memorial to Drake. They had asked the Duke of Bedford for help with money. He commissioned Joseph Boehm, a sculptor from Vienna, to make a statue. The people of Plymouth asked if they could have a replica as they had not collected enough money to commission one of their own.

The statue stands on a pedestal of red Aberdeen granite. It is about 3m (10ft) high and made of bronze. Many people were disappointed that Drake is wearing the clothes of an Elizabethan man of rank and not uniform. Some say he was not as handsome as the statue portrays, but it is considered a work of art.

The defeat of the Spanish Armada was the first historical event for which medals were struck by an English sovereign.

c 1540
Francis Drake born near Tavistock, Devon
1577
Began world voyage
1581
Drake knighted on board *Golden Hind*
1588
Defeat of Spanish Armada
1596
Drake died
1880
Memorial proposed marking 300th anniversary of round the world voyage
1884
Statue unveiled on Plymouth Hoe

Eros

1885
Lord Shaftesbury died
1886
Shaftesbury Avenue opened
1893
Eros unveiled
1923-28
Eros moved to Embankment Gardens while underground excavated
1932
Alfred Gilbert knighted
1939-47
Eros moved to wartime storage
1984
Statue removed for restoration
1986
Eros returned to Piccadilly Circus

Anthony Ashley Cooper, later 6th Earl of Shaftesbury, who is commemorated by the statue of Eros and Shaftesbury Avenue.

The statue known as Eros in the middle of Piccadilly Circus in London is in fact the Angel of Christian Charity. It was unveiled as the Shaftesbury Memorial Fountain to commemorate the 6th Earl of Shaftesbury. Shaftesbury Avenue which leads off Piccadilly Circus is named after him.

Lord Shaftesbury was involved in many good causes. He is best remembered as the social reformer who did much to help factory and mine workers. They had worked under appalling conditions. He also helped to get lunatics treated better and for poor children to have free education.

Money for the memorial was raised by public subscription. The sculptor chosen was Alfred Gilbert. He proposed a statue of a winged angel with a bow - a figure of love sending out missiles of kindness to symbolise Lord Shaftesbury's achievements. He made the statue of aluminium. At the time it was the largest figure made in this material. It was meant to stand above large bronze fountains. The memorial committee insisted that the fountains should contain drinking water so they were made smaller and never fully turned on as they would have soaked anyone trying to drink from them.

When the statue was first unveiled, many people were shocked by the figure of a naked boy put up in memory of such a great man. However, it became a familiar landmark and was known as Eros, the god of love. It was moved when the underground station at Piccadilly was built and again during the Second World War. The steps leading up to the statue have become a famous meeting place and it is boarded up for New Year's Eve celebrations to avoid damaging it.

Piccadilly Circus, at the heart of London's West End, has always been a popular meeting place for for Londoners and visitors.

Cenotaph

1914-18
First World War
1919
Temporary memorial erected as saluting point for victory march
1920
Cenotaph rebuilt in Portland stone
1939-45
Second World War
1946
Inscription relating to Second World War added

The word cenotaph means a memorial to the dead who are buried elsewhere. The Cenotaph which stands in London's Whitehall was first built in plaster by Sir Edwin Lutyens. The Imperial War Graves Commission wanted a memorial for all those who died abroad and which could be put up in time for the Allied 'Victory March' on 19 July 1919.

The temporary cenotaph was so widely admired for its simple design that a copy was made in Portland stone in time for the anniversary of Armistice Day on 11 November 1920. The Tomb of the Unknown Warrior in Westminster Abbey was built at the same time. Armistice Day on 11 November 1918 marked the end of the First World War. Armistice means a truce - an agreement to stop hostilities and to discuss peace terms.

Armistice Day has now become known as Remembrance Sunday and falls on the second Sunday in November. Artificial red poppies are worn to mark the day. A service is held in front of the Cenotaph to honour those who died in the First and Second World Wars. It is attended by members of the Royal Family, leaders of the political parties and people from the armed services. Wreaths made of poppies are laid at the base of the memorial and at 11 am there is a two-minute silence to honour all those who lost their lives.

The Cenotaph is a simple pillar which is narrower at the top. It has no religious symbols on it because it was meant to honour men and women of all beliefs. The only decorations on it are the flags of the three armed services and the Merchant Navy. The dedication reads 'To the Glorious Dead'.

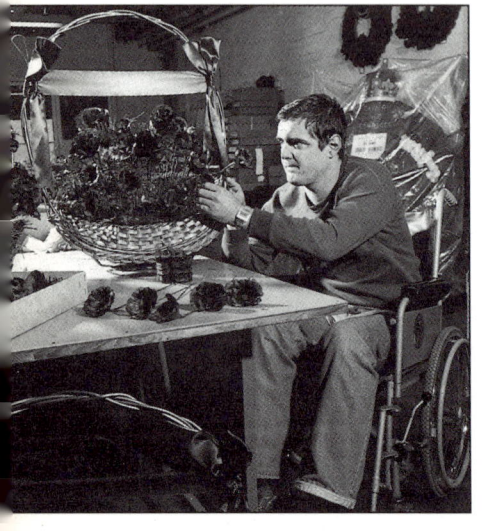

Disabled servicemen traditionally make the red poppies which are associated with Remembrance Sunday. Poppies grew on the battlefields where many people died.

The Cenotaph, a memorial to those who died and are buried elsewhere.

Churchill's Statue

1874
Winston Churchill born at Blenheim Palace
1901
Entered House of Commons
1908
Churchill married Clementine Hazier
1940-45
Served as head of wartime coalition government
1951
Became prime minister for second time
1953
Received knighthood
1955
Retired as prime minister
1965
Sir Winston Churchill died
1973
Statue unveiled

The statue of Sir Winston Churchill in Parliament Square in London is the national monument to one of the world's greatest statesmen. It is said that he chose the site himself in the early 1950s. He was shown plans for the redevelopment of Parliament Square by Sir David Eccles, the Minister of Works then, and put a circle in the north-east corner saying this was where his statue would go.

The bronze statue was unveiled in 1973 by Lady Spencer-Churchill accompanied by the Queen. It stands over 3.5m (12ft) high on a plinth nearly 2.5m (8ft) high. The only inscription is 'CHURCHILL'. It dwarfs the statues of other statesmen in the square. Sir Winston Churchill is portrayed wearing an army greatcoat and he faces the House of Commons where he served for 64 years. It was sculpted by Ivor Roberts-Jones who wanted to portray Churchill as the great leader who inspired the British during the Second World War and offered them only 'blood, toil, tears and sweat' in the struggle to keep their freedom.

The unveiling ceremony was attended by the Queen Mother, four generations of the Churchill family, the Prime Minister and former prime ministers and politicians. The square and approaches to it were crowded with people. The band of the Royal Marines played many of his favourite tunes.

As well as being prime minister for two terms, he was well-known as an artist and writer. He was made a Knight of the Order of the Garter in 1953, the same year he won the Nobel Prize for literature. He retired as prime minister in 1955 and refused to be made an earl or duke. He wanted to serve in the House of Commons.

The statue of Churchill as the great war leader. Around it are pictures of him as a boy of seven (**1**); at 19 at the Royal Military Academy at Sandhurst (**2**); at 25 as a soldier (**3**); at 34 when he married (**4**); at 36 when he was home secretary (**5**) and at 66 showing his famous victory salute (**6**).

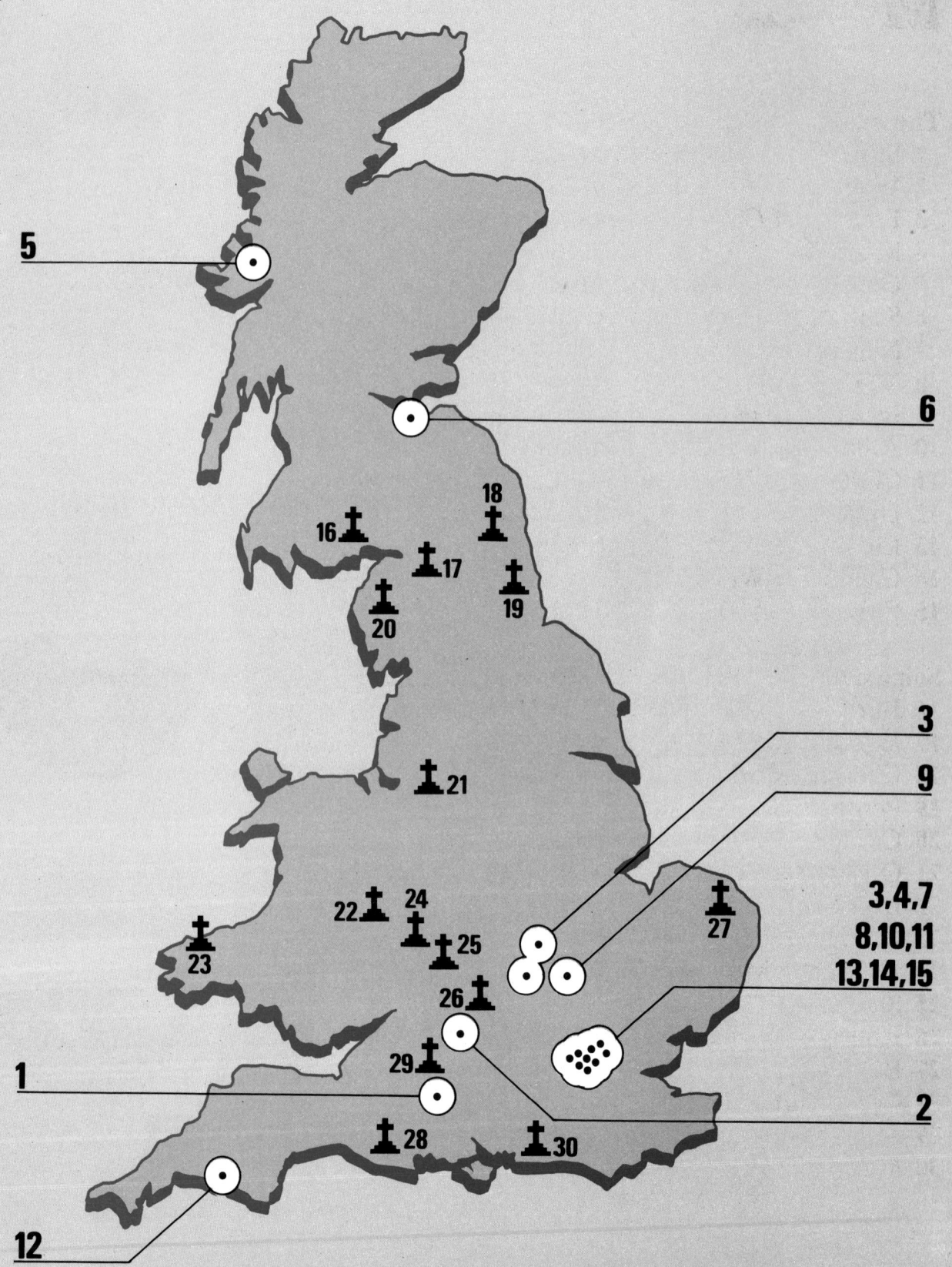

Monuments of interest

The monuments in this book
1. Stonehenge, Salisbury Plain, Wiltshire
2. White Horse of Uffington, Berkshire
3. Eleanor of Castile Crosses
4. Monument, Fish Street, London
5. Glenfinnan Monument, Highlands
6. Scott Monument, Edinburgh, Lothian
7. Nelson's Column, Trafalgar Square, London
8. Marble Arch, London
9. Ickwell Green Maypole, Bedfordshire
10. Albert Memorial, Kensington Gardens, London
11. Cleopatra's Needle, Embankment, London
12. Drake's Statue, Plymouth, Devon
13. Eros, Piccadilly Circus, London
14. Cenotaph, Whitehall, London
15. Churchill's Statue, Parliament Square, London

Some other interesting monuments
16. Burns' Statue and Mausoleum, Dumfries
17. Hadrian's Wall, Cumbria and Northumberland
18. Chester's Fort, Northumberland
19. Penshaw Monument, Durham
20. Castlerigg Stone Circle, Cumbria
21. Quarry Bank Mill, Wilmslow, Cheshire
22. Iron Bridge, Telford, Shropshire
23. Cerrig-y-Gof, Dyfed
24. Avoncroft Museum of Buildings, Bromsgrove, Hereford
25. Shakespeare's Birthplace, Stratford-upon-Avon, Warwickshire
26. Rollright Stones, Oxfordshire
27. Berney Arms Windmill, Norfolk
28. Cerne Abbas Giant, Dorset
29. Avebury Stone Circle, Wiltshire
30. Market Cross, Chichester, West Sussex

Types of monuments

1 Stone circles Nobody knows exactly when they were built but it is thought that they were places for religious occasions. The most famous is Stonehenge.
2 Burial mounds These were either round barrows or long ones. They were burial tombs built in the Bronze Age, 3000-1800 BC.
3 Cerne Abbas Giant Chalk-cut figures, including horses and crosses are a bit of a mystery. They had to be looked after and cleaned to stop grass growing over them.
4 Dolmens These were Neolithic stones which formed burial chambers.
5 Memorial window Stained glass windows, like this one of St Thomas at Canterbury, were often placed in windows of churches as a memorial to a person or event.
6 Statues Many cities have statues commemorating people. This one is of Queen Boudica in London.
7 Brasses Memorial brasses are often set in the wall or floor of a church, or graveyard.
8 Tombstone Some are very old like this Roman tombstone. Some of the later ones are very ornate and have elaborate carvings on them.

9 Royal Air Force Memorial There are many symbolic memorials like this one of an eagle spreading its wings as if it is about to fly off.
10 Triumphal arch Many cities have arches with statues on top to commemorate a person or event.
11 Martyrs' Memorial Monuments are often built to commemorate disasters. There are usually plaques describing the events.
12 Drumclog Monument Monuments marking the scene of battles and skirmishes can be found in many places throughout the country.
13 Market Cross All important towns had crosses at the centre on the main road by the town hall where local regulations were set out.
14 Horse trough Horse troughs and drinking fountains were a common sight before piped water was freely available.
15 Drinking fountain Some granite drinking fountains can still be seen in parks and gardens.
16 Park bench Many benches have brass plaques on them in memory of a person who either paid for the bench to be placed in a park for public use or who was known to have enjoyed sitting there.

Useful addresses

English Heritage
PO Box 43
Ruislip
Middlesex HA4 0XW
(Historic Buildings and Monuments Commission)
(Written enquiries only)

The National Trust
(for Places of Historic Interest or Natural Beauty)
36 Queen Anne's Gate
London SW1H 9AS
Tel: 01 222 9251

Society for the Protection of Ancient Buildings
37 Spital Square
London E1 6DY
Tel: 01 377 1644

English Tourist Board
4 Grosvenor Gardens
London SW1W 0DJ
Tel: 01 730 3400

Scottish Tourist Board
23 Ravelston Terrace
Edinburgh EH4 3EU
Tel: 031 332 2433

National Trust for Scotland
5 Charlotte Square
Edinburgh EH2 4DU
Tel: 031 226 5922

CADW Welsh Historic Monuments/Wales Tourist Board
Brunel House
2 Fitzalan Road
Cardiff CF2 1UY
Tel: 0222 499909

Association for Industrial Archaeology
The Wharfage
Ironbridge
Telford
Shropshire TF8 7AW
Tel: 095 245 3522

Index

Albert Memorial, 24-25
Alexander, Sir James, 26
Alexandria, 26
Alfred the Great, 8
Angel of Christian Charity, 30
Armada, 28-29
Armistice Day, 32
Aswan, 26
Augustus Caesar, 26
Bedford, Duke of, 29
Boehm, Joseph, 29
Bonnie Prince Charlie, 14-15
Buckingham Palace, 20
Cenotaph, The, 32-33
Charing Cross, 11-12
Charles II, King, 13
Churchill's Statue, 34-35
Cleopatra's Needle, 26-27
Commons, House of, 34
Cooper, Anthony Ashley, 30
Copenhagen, Battle of, 19
Culloden Moor, Battle of, 15
Dixon, John, 26
Dragon's Hill, 9
Drake's Statue, 28-29
Druids, 6
Eccles, Sir David, 34
Edward I, King, 10
Eleanor of Castile Crosses, 10-11
Elizabeth I, Queen, 28
Epona, 8
Eros, 30-31
Fire of London, the Great, 12-13
Fish Street, 12
Geddington, 10, 11
George IV, King, 20
Giant's Stairs, 9
Gilbert, Alfred, 30
Glenfinnan Monument, 14-15
Golden Hind, The, 28
Great Exhibition, 24
Great Fire of London, 12-13
Greenaway, Kate, 22
Harby, 10
Hardingstone, 10, 11
Heliopolis, 26
Holyroodhouse, 14
Hooke, Robert, 12
House of Commons, 34
Ickwell Green Maypole, 22-23
Imperial War Graves Commission, 32

John of Battle, 11
Kemp, George Meikle, 16
Kensington Gardens, 24
King's Troop Royal Horse Artillery, 20-21
Landseer, Sir Edwin, 18, 19
Loch Shiel, 14
Lutyens, Sir Edwin, 32
Macdonald, Alexander, 15
Maida, 16
Marble Arch, 20-21
May Day, 22-23
Medals, 29
Monument, The, 12-13
Morris dancers, 23
Nash, John, 20
Nelson's Column, 18-19
Nile, Battle of the, 19
Northill, 22
Old Warden, 22
Pelican, The, 28
Piccadilly Circus, 30-31
Plymouth, 28-29
Poppies, 32
Prestonpans, 14
Prince Albert, 24-25
Princes Street, 16
Pudding Lane, 12
Railton, William, 18
Remembrance Sunday, 32
Roberts-Jones, Ivor, 34
Royal Society, 13
St Finnan's Isle, 14
St George, 9
St Paul's Cathedral, 18
St Vincent, Battle of, 19
Salisbury Plain, 6
Scott, Sir George Gilbert, 24
Scott Monument, 16-17
Shaftesbury, 6th Earl of, 30
Spanish Armada, 28-29
Speakers' Corner, 21
Spencer-Churchill, Lady, 34
Steell, Sir John, 16
Stonehenge, 6-7
Stuart, Prince Charles Edward, 14-15
Suicides, 13
Thames Embankment, 26-27
Tomb of the Unknown Warrior, 32
Torel, William, 11
Trafalgar, Battle of, 18, 19
Trilithons, 6-7
Tyburn, 20-21

Uffington White Horse, 8-9
Upper Caldecote, 22
Victoria, Queen, 24-25
Waltham Cross, 10, 11
Waverley novels, 16
White Horse of Uffington, 8-9
William of Ireland, 11
Wilson, Erasmus, 27
Wren, Sir Christopher, 12-13

HOUSES

WOBURN

HAMPTON COURT

BEAULIEU

BURGHLEY

LONGLEAT

HATFIELD

HOLYROODHOUSE

CASTLE HOWARD

BLENHEIM

BROADLANDS

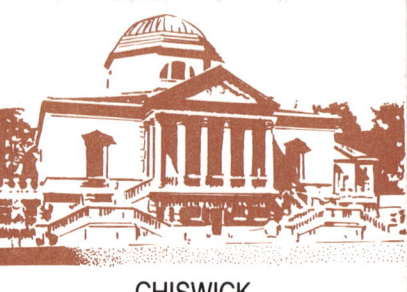
CHISWICK

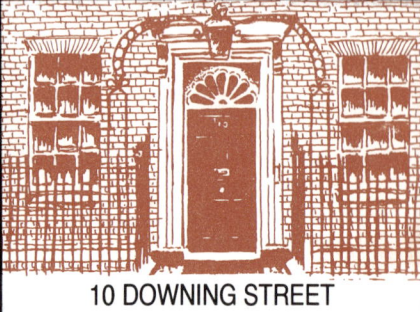
10 DOWNING STREET

HAREWOOD

ROYAL PAVILION

BUCKINGHAM PALACE